TBD

A journey through pain, healing, and self-love

Coral Stewart

MILTON & HUGO L.L.C.
4407 Park Ave., Suite 5
Union City, NJ 07087, USA

Website: *www. miltonandhugo.com*
Hotline: *1- 888-778-0033*
Email: *info@miltonandhugo.com*

Ordering Information:
Quantity sales. Special discounts are granted to corporations, associations, and other organizations. For more information on these discounts, please reach out to the publisher using the contact information provided above.

Library of Congress Control Number:		2025917024
ISBN-13:	979-8-89285-593-8	[Paperback Edition]
	979-8-89285-591-4	[Hardback Edition]
	979-8-89285-594-5	[Digital Edition]

Rev. date: 07/28/2025

Dedications

Dedicated to Brandy, Logan, and Rayne Warne.
My Aunts and Uncles, thank you for inspiring
me and helping me along this journey.
To my best friend and biggest fan, Rosemary.
You will always be my family.
I would also like to thank the high school teachers
who supported me and made this achievement
possible. Mrs. Wright and Mr. White, thank
you for giving me a safe space to dream.

You don't have to read this.

You don't have to buy it.

You don't even have to touch it.

But please,

Allow me to write it.

Allow me to, for one fleeting moment,

Open my wounds and bleed ink onto these pages.

Because this black sap is mixing with the red

And these words are being embedded into my skin

I need to get them out.

Not for you,

But for my own sanity.

So give me these pages to cleanse my body's blood

And erase the writing on my arms.

…

But feel free to buy it.

Contents

Pain

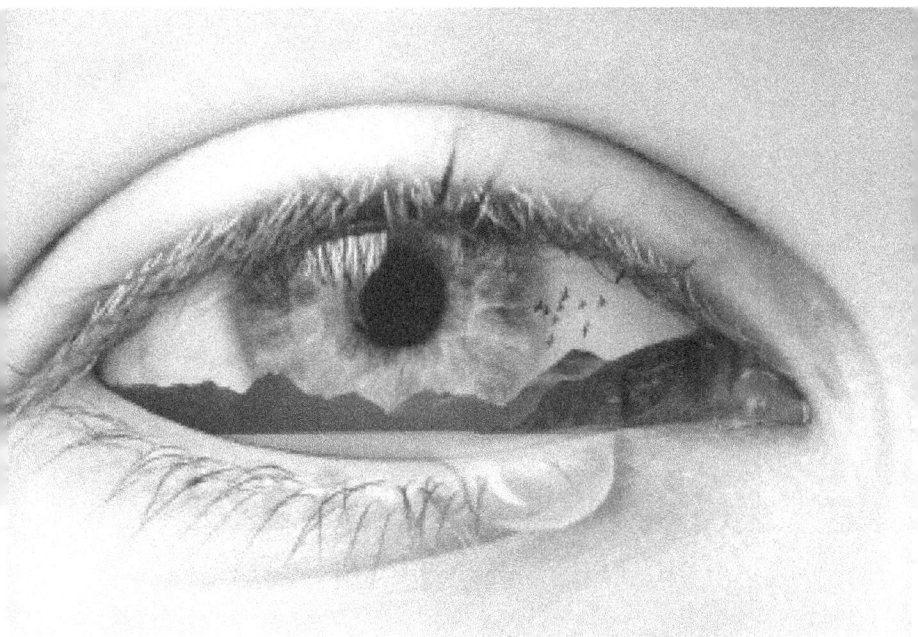

Just don't

Just don't
Don't cry over my final words
Because I've said all I needed to say
Don't cry over my last song
It was never meant to play
And don't cry over my last breath
Because I bet it wasn't long
Just don't cry over my death
Because I was already gone

I'm not "mature for my age".

I'm traumatized.

I'm screaming
Can you hear me?
Counting in my head
1
2
3
Maybe they will hear me now
I scream again
It just comes back to me
The darkness swallows my cries
It does not want me to escape
But I want to
I'm banging on the glass
Can you see me?
I see you
Walking right past as the tears fall down my face
But you do not see
I'm begging on the floor
Can you help me?
Please help me

I'm happy
I sing from the depths of my soul on a
stage, and look out at my fans

I'm happy
I skip through downtown with my best
friend and a cup of coffee

I'm happy
I go out to a party and move to the
music, surrounded by the people I love

I'm angry
I scream profanities at a wall because it
dared to stub my toe

But I'm happy!
I play a board game with my aunt and uncle
and laugh so hard I snort

I'm happy
I mean, I got an A on my
chemistry test

I'm sad
I cry on the floor of the school bathroom
because my hair tie broke

No, I'm happy!
I smile and pump my fists in the back of a crowded car
to a song I don't even know

I'm angry
I punch a pillow because my brother
used the outlet I wanted to use

I'm sad
I take a shower in the dark because the running
water drowns out my sobs

But I'm happy now
I have a party with all my friends

…

I think I'm happy

…

Why aren't I happy?

…

I'm not happy.
I'm just distracting myself from the depression.

I miss me.

You might have expected a poem, but that's all I've got.
I miss me.

Fake

You would never have known her smile was tainted
Unless you painted it yourself
You would never have known her laugh was forced
Unless you held it in its jail
You would never have known her sparkly eyes
Were from the endless nights she cried
Unless you knew her for what she was
And the monster that lived inside

I loved you before I knew how to.
And that was the most unfair part of it all.

I've been writing for years now,

Taking every aspect of my life and putting it on paper.

Morphing it into a story I could read

Over and over again,

Until I no longer needed to.

But there was one thing I could never get myself to write.

One thing where every time I tried,

The pencil wouldn't connect with the paper.

And the truth is,

I don't know how to write it

Saying you hurt me isn't enough.

Saying you took something,

Or broke something,

Doesn't give justice to what you did

The word *pain*

Never described what I felt

Horrifying,

Can't describe what happened.

But maybe that's ok

Maybe I'll just keep it right next to me,

Tucked away in my little box of trauma,

Until it can make its way onto the page.

Love is fake
Romance is a lie
I'll be lonely
Until the day I die

It might not make sense to you,

Why I say I'm okay when I'm not,

And it doesn't have to.

I say that because you can't help me.

You can't fix the problems that I have

And too many people have asked me that, and not wanted the honest answer.

Too many times,

People have given me empty promises and void apologies

And it's happened enough for it to just not be worth anymore.

No one knows the battle I fight inside
of me every day

No one can see the darkness I carry, because the light of
my smile coats it like a funeral veil.

I keep it bright and burning for those who need
it, without even realizing,
I am the one who needs it the most.

There is a reason they call it
"Falling in love"
I fell hard,
And I broke.

You don't see my tears or my pain.
You don't see my darkness,
Or the broken heart I hide.
But you see my mistakes.

...

That's all you see.

Trauma

I remember screaming
And fighting
Feeling hopeless to stop it
I remember drowning
And crying
Biting my lip until it bled
I was supposed to forget
But I didn't
I remember

…

Why can't I forget?

I don't know

I'm happy
I'm sad
I'm calm
I'm mad
I'm up
I'm down
I smile
I frown
I'm tired
I'm awake
I like brownies
I like cake
I'm hot
I'm cold
I'm young
I'm old
I'm going crazy
Can't make up my mind
The one thing I know
Is that I want to cry

Do you know what it's like to scream
and nobody hear you?

If you do, I'm sorry

How am I supposed to tell you how I feel when I don't know myself?

How am I supposed to describe a feeling that I don't have?

How am I supposed to be ok when I don't know how?

Why can't someone just tell me what to do?

Why can't someone hold my hand and help me up?

Why do I have to pick up my broken pieces?

I want them to pick me up.

To take me into their hands,

And put me back together, gently.

I don't even know how I fell apart

I don't remember the fall

Just hitting the ground

I don't remember what I was like before.

Before the numb set in

Happy I guess

Why did it leave?

Where did my happiness go?

Please let her know I'm looking for her

I miss her.

I'm in Pain.

I'm in pain when you can't see it.
I'm in pain when I say I'm ok
I'm in pain when I'm smiling.
I have a chronic illness.
I am always in pain.

I'm angry, and sad, and I feel disconnected.

I feel alone and like nobody would miss me if I were gone.

I don't want to die,

I just don't want to do this anymore.

I'm scared.

I don't like this monster inside of me,

It's not who I am,

But it's taking over.

My best friend in the entire world is barely acknowledging my existence.

I love him to death, but I shouldn't,

It's stupid.

He saved my life and kept me going, and now,

I don't even know him anymore.

I'm alone.

I just want someone to notice.

I want someone to look into my eyes and know I'm hurting.

To hold me,

And love me,

And tell me I'm going to be ok.

I'm so messed up.

I stutter and struggle to move and talk when I'm upset.

I'm crazy.

I don't deserve friends,

That's why I don't have any.

I don't deserve a partner either,

Who could ever love someone like me?

I'm so difficult.

No wonder he stopped talking to me.

I wish all this pain would go away.

But maybe I deserve it.

I don't know.

I'm alone.

I'm scared.

Send help

To Be Seen

I know that if I tell them,
They will care.
That if I say,
"Hey, I'm in pain."
They will listen.
But I can't.
Every time I try,
The words get caught in my throat, and I can't speak.
And maybe,
I don't want to have to tell them.
Maybe, I want someone to notice.
I want someone to see my messy room and not get mad,
But ask me if I'm all right.
Someone who notices me spacing out and doesn't just laugh it off,
But asks me what's on my mind.
Someone who cares enough,
Who knows me enough,
To see the little things.
I want to be seen.

Teenager

I remember being a kid
How I couldn't wait until I woke up,
To see the sunshine and the early birds chirp
To start new adventures within the safety of my boundaries
every day.
Now I'm a teenager,
And I'm wondering when I can go back to sleep.

Candy

A little kid walking through the jungles of a grocery store
He sees mountains filled to the brim with every sweet and
salty treat he could dream of
His mother
Clinging to his hand in order not to lose him
He stays on the path until something
Catches his eye
A treat wrapped in shiny gold paper, tied with a single
pink bow
I want that one!
But he hears a no.
The grocery clerk has now stepped in
It's my candy. It is not for sale.
But it was right there!
So shiny and perfect, just waiting to be eaten
It was practically asking for it.
So he takes it
He's not a thief, he is merely taking what he deserves.
If she didn't want to give it, why did it look so pretty?
So beautiful.
Well, I was not made to be beautiful

I was not made for you to pick out and claim
You are not a toddler, and I am not some pretty good you get
to grab
I wrap myself in gold because I am just as precious.
Wanting something does not mean you are entitled to it
Why do men feel they are entitled to my body?
Entitled to take something the second it isn't given.
I am not some prize sitting on a shelf, waiting for you to
notice me
Waiting to be picked,
To be chosen,
To be taken.
I don't remember signing away the deeds to my body, so why
act as if you own them?
It is called 'Predator' because you prey on the ones you deem
weak.
Children whose eyes shine with innocence
Teens who are not taught to be afraid of
And grown women who are beaten, manipulated, and
drugged
For one night of his satisfaction.
We are then left in the dust, missing a piece of ourselves we
will never get back.

And you take that piece and you wear it as a medal around your neck

As if it were not a fragment of a taken bright soul simply because you chose her

Because the princesses are waiting to be chosen.

To be saved.

Well, let me tell you something

I saved myself a long time ago when it was the prince who left me broken

When we are taught as kids

That the boy who pulled our hair and threw us in the mulch,

Liked us,

How can you expect us to see the signs?

You would never blame the candy for being stolen.

So don't blame the woman for being raped.

"What does Chronic illness feel like?"

It feels like my body is at war with itself, and I'm not even on the battlefield.

I don't care if I'm a warrior.

I don't care if I'm the strongest person you've ever met.

I worked for this strength,

I fought for it.

I fought battles that I didn't want to fight,

Battles I didn't know how to fight.

I don't want to be a warrior.

I want to be a kid.

Tired

When you ask me what's wrong,
And I say
"I'm tired",
I don't mean sleep tired.
I mean, I'm tired of feeling like this
I'm tired of working my ass into the ground
I'm tired of panic attacks that make me vomit
I'm tired of not being able to stop the tears once they come
I'm tired of pretending everything's alright
I'm tired of the impossible standards I am held to
I'm tired of doing everything for everyone else
I'm tired of not being able to clean my room
I'm tired of how difficult it is to take my meds
I'm tired of worrying about my blood sugar.
I'm just tired.
I don't need sleep,
I need grace.

The Truth

Roses aren't always red
And violets aren't even blue
The world that we live in
Doesn't like to tell the truth
Smiles aren't always happy
And laughs aren't always real
Sometimes the scars are hidden
And sometimes they're something we feel
The person who smiles the brightest
Is the one who cries the most
And the person who gives the best advice
Once felt like they were toast
And the person who is always happy
Knows what it's like to always be sad
And the person who laughs the most
Knows it's just all an act
And above all the others
We have the person who's the most help
Because they were the person
Who had to walk through hell.

Fire Extinguisher

It's a different kind of pain
When the one person who said they would never leave
Left.
The person who said they would always answer your late 911
calls
Stopped picking up.
The one friend,
Who promised to hold your hand and walk through the fire
together forever
Ran when the flames got too big.
Why?
They were supposed to be your one and only,
Your ride or die,
Your fire extinguisher.
But I guess you learn
Even the fire extinguishers,
Go up in flames.

I don't want to be a warrior
I didn't choose this life
To hold a sword instead of a pen
To strike the demons instead of the walls
I didn't want it to be like this.
I wasn't ready to spend my life fighting.
I want to sing,
And dance,
And play.
Be a kid again.
But I don't get that luxury.
Instead,
You will find me here.
Wringing the blood out of my clothes,
Wiping my brow,
And getting ready for my next battle.

Water Kid

When I was a kid
My idea of broken was a lamp that had fallen from the height
of your nightstand,
Or a crispy cookie snapped in two and suddenly wasn't worth
it anymore.
I never imagined broken could be used to describe the
delicate mind of a human,
Or the rage boiling out of a beaten soul.
Growing up
I watched everyone place a minor inconvenience into the
category of being broken.
Oh, you dropped a line?
Broken.
You didn't get an A on that test?
Broken.
You can't fit into that skirt?
You must be broken.
Soon,
It went from society screaming that phrase at me every
second I walked through the door,
To my own mind, reminding me of it every day.

You dropped that line on stage?

Broken.

You didn't get an A on that test?

Broken.

You can't fit into that skirt?

It's because you're broken!

Slowly,

The true part of me watched from afar as I was consumed by the longing to be whole,

To be perfect

Oh, they're known for their burgers? …

Let's go with the salad

Looks delicious, but let me just add it up.

Yes, I would like a cookie, but I want to fit into that prom dress

I wanted to believe I was fixing myself,

That I was gluing my broken pieces back together,

But in reality,

I could feel myself falling apart.

The gaps between my shattered edges expanded as the gap between my waist and pants grew with them,

So much pain for one "You're beautiful," as if their words were the center of my universe

My whole life leading up to the moment they told me they
liked what they saw
But it taught me how to act
To plaster on a smile and say
No, thank you, I'm not hungry—
When my stomach was trying to digest the mere image of it
So many dizzy spells and weak legs, trying to stay focused on
logarithms,
And so many months spent learning that beautiful is what I
make it,
And, perfect does not exist.
One day, you're not hungry.
The next,
You're broken.
But it's hard to realize you have a problem when the only
acknowledgments are compliments:
A triple zero waist!—how did you do it?!
I would look them in the eyes and tell them I'm sick, but they
would just shake their heads
No, they would say:
You're beautiful.

I wish I could have their eyes.

They see a perfect waist,
I see a pouch.
They see a button nose,
I see a pointy one.
They see beautiful and happy, and whole.
I   see   broken.
Because I have an addiction,
Not to popping amphetamines,
Or a nicotine high
But to the piercing cold rush of water hitting the bottom of
an empty well,

But, at least I can act, right?

Healing

People asked me when it stopped

All the hurting

But the truth is

The pain never really went away

I greeted it at the door to my heart like an old friend

I took the pain and I'll continue to every day

Because to feel pain is to live

And I would rather be alive in pain,

Then dead in the numb.

214

I remember coming back to school and people asking me
where I had been
What I was doing.
My mind immediately flipped back to Thanksgiving with my
family
Everyone gathered around a big table,
Passing the turkey, cranberry sauce, and pumpkin pie
Walking through the door with glass dishes
Lightly covered by tin foil
A big smile on their faces,
Excited to share the food they loved with the people they
loved.
And I remember holding my phone just below the table
So I could Google the calories in mashed potatoes
214.
I remember inspecting every bite of ham to be sure there was
no fat on it
Re-arranging the food on my plate so it looks like I ate more
And I remember people noticing, and stopping only to talk
about my
"Weird quirks"
But I knew something they didn't.

At least

A part of me buried very, very deep did

I knew that it was screaming at me you're sick! But I couldn't

hear it over the numbers

How do I answer that question?

What have I been doing?

How do you tell people you're sick when you have no virus

When it forms from thoughts in your head

How do you tell people the truth when the truth is

You were fighting for your life against a monster inside of you

Having to fight every urge in your body just to eat a piece of

pizza

How do you fight the monster when you have no weapons?

You scream.

You scream the truth against it because the monster is made

of lies

Lies like a piece of a cake will make you gain five pounds

That the pain is coming from eating too much, not too little

That your beauty is determined by your size.

But I am done seeking revenge on my body for being

different

My stomach was not made for you to look at in a bikini

My jiggly thighs allow me to walk,

And run,

And dance!

My boobs, that are too big for your comfort, were not made to comfort you.

These curves are not made for you to have an opinion on

Because I am a woman.

And I am beautiful.

So, how do I answer their question?

I say I came back from war.

I Loved You Then and I Love You Now

I remember the day we met
It was love at first sight
The thought of you and me together
Well, it just felt right
They all said I was crazy
And to be honest, I probably was
But they can't deny my feelings
Because I knew I was in love
Over the many years
My feelings grew and grew
All I wanted was one thing
All I ever wanted was you
And when that love song played
And you asked me to dance
That's when I knew for sure
I was going to give you a chance
I always knew it was just me
With all the love in my heart
Even though it hurt so bad, I didn't want us to part
I dealt with all the pain
Because it was better than losing you

Heartbreak hurts like hell
But I'm glad our friendship grew
It kills me every day
Knowing we can't be more
But I'm not sure I locked it
That ever-tempting door
So when they ask about my love for you
I say even more than you can count
Because the only thing I've always known
I loved you then, and I love you now

I don't just want a relationship.
I don't just want to be loved.
I want to be seen.

I'm not sure if I fell in love with him,

Or the way he made me feel.

He was the first guy,

Outside of my uncles,

Who ever made me feel safe.

Like it didn't matter when or if I fell,

He would always catch me.

I knew that if I let down my guard and held out my hand,

I wouldn't have to worry about what he would do.

I didn't trust him blindly,

But I could trust him with my eyes closed.

No farewell words were spoken
There was no time to say goodbye
You left without us knowing
And only god knows why
I now grow up in a world
That you aren't in
It hurts a lot sometimes
But crying's not a sin
It's always ok to be sad
And miss the ones you love
But they can still see you
They watch you from above
And even though I have
To live my life without you
I shouldn't miss out on what is here
Because it will go away too
So when I feel like crying
And you're not here to hold me tight
I promise I'll keep going
Through day and the night
Because you will always hold
A special place in my heart
And because of God's love,
We will never truly part.

Teach me

I don't know much about love,

I'm not very good at it.

But what I do know,

Is that you make me happier than anyone has ever made me

And I know that every morning when I wake up,

I look at my phone, hoping for a message from you

And that I think about you

And want to be with you

All the time

And if that means that I love you,

Then I love you.

And that scares me more than death itself.

Because I don't know how to love someone without hurting them

But you,

You make me want to learn

So, please.

Teach me.

Give me a chance.

I don't want to die,

Existing is just hard right now.

The Voice of a Woman. Written by a Woman.

We never said not to compliment us.
We love compliments.
"Hey, I just wanted to say you're really pretty"
Thank you, that's so sweet!
"Hey, baby, your rack looks great in that dress"
Is that supposed to make me blush?
Or sometimes you get the good old-fashioned whistle.
You walk around whistling, and hollering,
Like our bodies were made for your pleasure.
Our bodies,
Were made only to hold the exquisite soul of a woman.

"Quiet down, you're talking too loud"
I'm passionate, ok?
You don't get to silence us,
You've had your turn to speak for centuries.
Since the beginning of time, everything was handed to men,
While we watched you take everything from us.
You took our rights.
You took our voice.

You took our bodies as if they were your own.

"Boys will be boys you know"
And what is a boy exactly?
A knight in shining armor, come to save the princess?
Well I don't see a damsel in distress.
Do you?
If boys will be boys,
Then women get to be women.
And we're gonna decide what that label is, not society.
Screw society!
It's our turn to speak,
And this time,
You are gonna be the ones to shut up and listen.
Because I'm tired of holding my tongue while you run yours.

"Well why isn't there anything promoting boy power"
Because you've always had power.
And you don't need silly little things to remind you you have
a place in this world.
Boys are handed the mics, while it's up to us to be heard.
This isn't our cry for help,
It's a demand for justice.

"Women are fragile"
But nothing is broken more easily than a man's pride.
They go to any lengths necessary,
To defend the actions of their brothers

"You can't put a steak in front of a lion and expect the lion
not to eat it"
That one's true,
But it doesn't apply.
Because here's the difference,
The meat was made for the lion, and the lion was made to eat
meat.
But women, weren't made for sex.
They weren't made to be raped.

Oh I'm sorry,
Did that word make you uncomfortable?
Well I've gotten pretty familiar with it.
Because we women are taught from a young age how to not
get raped.
How come we don't teach boys to not rape?

"Feminism is anti-men"
It's really not.
Feminism is not a strong, hateful word against men
It's what the world needs to heal itself.

And finally,
"Just say no"
Seems simple enough right?
Well, we tried.
You murdered us.

Sometimes

Sometimes
I need to remind myself that recovery
Isn't a straight line
Sometimes
I need to give myself a little grace to mess up
Sometimes
I need to be ok with not being ok
The low times make the high times worth it
And just because I'm not happy,
Doesn't mean I'm sad
When you've been through what I've gone through,
And you have the struggles that I have,
It's ok to simply exist.
Not every moment has to be filled with laughter or tears
It's ok to be in between.
It's ok to not know how to feel
Sometimes
It's ok to just be breathing.

You know that moment

When you draw a hot bath

And you sit in it

Waiting for it to fill up and cover you in its warmth

And once it does,

You tip your head back,

And allow your eyes to fall below the surface.

And for that moment,

For that mere moment,

It's quiet.

No outside noise,

No pain,

Just your heart beating inside your head.

I cherish those moments

Those fleeting seconds in life where I just simply exist.

I cherish them.

But sooner than later,

I must bring my head out of the water,

And come back to life.

"Are you good?"

No. But I'm ok. If there's anything I learned about myself it's that I'm not gonna be good every day. Some days I'm just ok. And that's alright.

My story

I don't care what they say
One day, I am going to change the world
And this will all just be a part of my story.
Words and sentences that make up my whole life
But how can some scribbles on a page summarize what I've
gone through
They can't.
In all of the 200,000 words in the English language,
None of them are deep enough to make you feel what I felt
Sadness doesn't explain the ache of losing someone you held
dear
Anger doesn't explain the rage of having your own life be
controlled
And loneliness doesn't explain the feeling that no one would
miss you if you were gone
But still.
I will try.
I will continue to write my pain out and share it with others
To allow them to use it as a stepping stone in their own
journey
But writing about the past can only do so much
Yes, this is my story.
One with bends and loops and forks and sometimes giant
cliffs,
But it's not quite done yet.

Every good book has an ending, and mine is still being
written
All I can do now
Is live in the moment.
Take the present one step at a time
Looking back every once in a while just to make sure it's all
still there,
And never looking too far ahead.
After all,
You can't write your future.
Destiny has always been the best storyteller.

Today, tomorrow, and the rest of my life

I may not know what happy looks like yet,
But I'm getting there.
It's enough for me to just not be sad.
For right now,
I'm ok with being ok
because that means I did it.
That means I lived,
I survived.
Today, I'm ok.
Tomorrow, I'm good.
And for the rest of my life, I'm better.

I did it.

I cut you out.

I kept you at a distance,

Pushed you as far as I could,

And I was good.

I was ok,

I was even happy.

But all it took was one text.

One text later and I'm a goner

I know I shouldn't have any expectations but god how could

I not

I love you with everything I have

We're perfect for each other!

How do you not see it?

It's right there

Right in front of you,

As clear as day.

I'm right in front of you.

See me

Please.

I'm here

I've been here for six years

I've been your best friend

I've been your escape
I've been your exception.
And I love that,
But can't I be something else?
How is it that every time I think im over you,
I just fall back in love
Over and over again
It's like my heart doesn't know anything but you
God I wish it did
This isn't easy
It's not easy to love you.
Actually,
It is
It's easy to love your big brown eyes
The way you run your fingers through your hair
Your big bright smile.
The way you support me like no one else has
The way you speak in that low voice when you're serious,
God, I light on fire.
So yeah,
It's easy to love you.
What's not easy,
Is for you to not love me back.
Not like that.
How do you not see it?

Everyone else does

I'm not sure if it's just because we're soulmates and my soul doesn't want to give up,

Or if I'm just cursed to an entirety of an unrequited love.

I don't know,

But please let it be the former.

True Love

Rock can bruise
And water can wear
Wind can chill
And fire turns forests bare
There is power
In what you see
But the most powerful thing
Lives inside you and me
It lives in our hearts
It lives in our souls
It comes from confidence
It asks us to be bold
Few people find it
The love that is true
But trust me I saw it
In her and you
It was valuable trust me
As shiny as gold
It lasted through the times
The young and old
It sometimes would bend
But it never broke
Even when death came
In his black cloak
She fought and she fought

But God called her home
We'll see her again
That I know
But love isn't temporary
At least the love that is true
You promised her that
When you said I do
It's okay to be sad
But your love is not lost
She's doing better now
Just at our cost
You know she would tell you
To just be strong
She could handle all this
She was never wrong
And though your love
Is stretched far overseas
She lives on
Inside you and me
So when you can't remember
Her smile or face
Remember her love
Cause it can't be replaced

The Dark Against the Light

When my happiness was falling into the pit of despair,
When depression's slender hands were gripping it tightly,
It cried out.
It thrust one hand into the darkness to try and find some light,
And it did.
It found you.
You kept my happiness alive,
You kept it glowing.
You kept me alive.
And so I'll take one more step out of the darkness.
And another,
And another.
I'll always keep on walking,
As long as you're by my side,
And we can spend our eternity in the light together.

I know it was mutual.

I know we agreed that it was for the best.

But if anything,

That makes it even harder.

It would be easier to hate you

To throw darts at a picture of your face and tell everyone how you did me wrong

It would be easier to be angry

To scream into a bowl of ice cream and block your number on my phone

It would be easier if you had hurt me

So I could justify these feelings of sadness

But you didn't.

You didn't do anything wrong.

We just wanted different things and that's what makes it so hard.

I don't feel anger or shame or betrayal,

I just feel loss.

The loss of someone I loved.

Someone that made me happy.

I constantly have to remind myself that we did the right thing and I wonder,

Do you do the same?

Do I creep into your mind at night the way you do mine?
I walk around like a zombie while you seem happy and busy
with your friends
Did it mean more to me than it did to you?
Was all the talk of you 'winning life' with me, just talk?
But alas I'll never know.
And I guess
It is what it is.

I don't know how to love halfway.
Once my toes touch the water,
And it's warm,
I dive right in,
Not even looking how deep.
Sometimes my feet hit the bottom too fast,
But I would rather risk the deep
Than live in the shallows.

Beyond the Numbers

I was not made to be beautiful
I am not broken nor breakable
I am simply a girl fighting a battle I didn't know how to fight
A battle that consumed every day of my life until I had
nothing left.
But I won't let my eating disorder define me.
Because that's not who I am
And that's not who I want to be
I may be figuring out who I am but I know what I'm not
I'm not judgy
I'm not weak
I'm not selfish
And I am not my eating disorder.
I am whoever I want to be.
And I want to be a girl who goes after what she wants,
A girl who stands up for herself and others,
A girl who doesn't care about the way her pants fit or how
others view her body
Because that's the real me.
Someone who is compassionate

And strong

And fucking awesome!

So I am going to take that step into recovery

Because I want to get better

I want to discover who I really am

Beyond the numbers

There are no pictures on these pages,
There are no drawings.
I did that on purpose.
These words occupy my brain,
So they will occupy your page.

They don't tell you how difficult Chronic illness is gonna be.

They don't tell you about the stigma and the impossible expectations you are held to.

They don't tell you that every day you just get more and more tired of it.

We're expected to get used to it,

To power through,

To be ok.

And while a lot of times we can be,

That's not gonna be every day.

It's ok to give yourself time and space to get better.

People with Chronic illness have different limitations than healthy people

And that needs to be normalized.

So if you're struggling with Chronic Illness, this is what I have to say to you:

This sucks.

It's not fun.

It's hard.

Some days you're better and some days you're not.

But that's alright.

Please give yourself grace.

You don't have to be so strong all the time.

It's ok to take a nap after work

Or wait one more day to fold that laundry.

Our lives are different
When others don't understand, it sucks,
But they don't need to.
Do what you have to do for you.
I wish someone had told me to.

Eventually

Eventually
She found peace
Eventually
She was able to laugh and dance and sing
Eventually
She was able to be happy and whole
Eventually
She was ok
But even though she is ok now
She doesn't forget
There is no eventually for the hours she spent crying
There is no eventually for the days she wondered if she would
make it through the night
They would be embedded in her past like stones in the forest
Her pain was forever a part of her
And she didn't hide it
She was never ashamed
For she knew
You can't always count on the eventually's

Speak to me
Of her memories
I truly want to know
Sing to me
All her melodies
So that I can learn and grow
Keep her memory alive
Spread it across the sea and sky
Send it on the breeze
Through the birds in the trees
So her legacy won't die with me

When I say I don't like her for you,
It's not because I want you for me.
It's because I see it written on your face
I see the unhappiness in your brow,
The pain behind your smile.
I want you to be free of her,
Not for me,
But for you.

Where there is no noise,

There is quiet.

Where there is no people,

There is space.

Where there are no thoughts,

There is peace.

I live in the places where there isn't.

The places not everyone can find,

But everyone can dream.

I live deep within the columns of my skull,

Waiting for all the noise,

And the people,

And the thoughts,

To disappear,

So I can emerge.

So I can emerge, and simply be.

What not to say to a disabled person

"You can do it despite your disability"

I don't do anything DESPITE my disability. I work WITH my disability to do it.

"Try being more positive. It will make you feel better about it"

I was denied a normal life by an illness I can't control. I am allowed to be upset about it.

"Maybe if you ate healthier…"

Food is something that can bring me a lot of joy, even though one of my illnesses causes me to have an allergy to gluten. I will eat what makes me happy.

"Try exercising more"

This is specific to those who still have at least some movement with their disability, but is still not helpful. If I need an aid to walk more than half a mile, I don't think going to the gym is the best idea.

"You just need to rest"

You are absolutely right, but resting can look like different things to different people. As long as you are healing your mind and body, rest can look like anything. So just don't put restrictions on it.

To the average person,

These are just pages.

To a reader,

They're an escape.

To a poet,

It's a journey.

But to me,

This is my story.

My heart, mind, and soul written in ink for you to see.

The years of my life fill these pages.

To me,

This is so much more than a book.

Than a collection of poems.

It is my healing.

So please,

Be careful with it.

Me

Quiet little garden

I sit under the maple
That reaches the sky
Listening to the dark crow's
Sad little cry
I feel the soft grass
Underneath my palm
One quick look
And your thoughts are gone
This quiet little garden
Looks soft and still
But if you listen closely
Just beyond the hills
You can hear the booms
Of the coming storm
But for now, I'm here
Safe and warm
So I hold my book
A little closer to my heart
For I won't leave
Until the sky turns dark
Because this quiet little garden
Tucked beneath the sky
Is my safe place
My place to hide

Each day I wake up and
Find a different way to love you

Simple and Sweet

I don't like to say I love you
To me
It doesn't say enough

How can three measly words
Thrown into the wind without a second thought
Truly convey what I feel for you

How can the word love
So simple and sweet
Be what we use when true love is anything but

True love is what we have
And our love
Is like watching a stormy ocean from its depths

It is the first chilling breeze in a domestic winter
The fire in the eye of the lion before it pounces
The fragrance of the wildflowers after the first spring rain

It is every fleeting moment in the universe that conveys
beauty
It's not about sparking one good feeling
But burning your nerves with every emotion you can feel
Love is not simple

Love is not sweet

Love is every miraculous thing in between

Nobody is "hard to love"
…
Loving is just hard.

The truth is

You scare me

The way you brush my arm when you laugh

Scares me

The way you look at me when you know I'm hurting

Scares me

The way you support me endlessly

Look out for me always

And trust me fiercely

Scares me

But the thought of losing you

Scares me so much

I crave the fear of knowing you

Wake me up

You can wake me up when my dreams become real
You can wake me up when happiness is something I feel
You can wake me up when fiction becomes the truth
You can wake me up only if I wake up next to you

When I choose to get out of bed in the morning,

When I am not so crippled by my illnesses that I can't even function,

I don't it because it's what's expected of me.

I don't do it because I was asked to.

I don't do it despite my disability.

I don't do it because there's nothing else I can do.

I do it because I deserve to live.

Because even though my life might look different than yours,

It is still a life.

I owe it to myself to live my days,

Whatever that may look like.

That could be using a wheelchair at the zoo.

It could be acting on a stage.

It could be writing from my couch when I can't walk around at school.

I am still living.

I am still surviving.

I am still thriving.

I might have a disability,

But I am.

Poetry

Is the rawest form of art us humans are capable of.

And poets,

Mere dancers in the light of it's beauty.

This is my love poem
Not to a boy or a world
But to me

I love the way my eyes sparkle when I laugh
The way my pinkie always lifts when I'm drinking
The way my hips sway as I walk

I love how I chew on my lip when I'm thinking
How my eyes get stormy when I'm upset
How I will always stand up for what I believe in

I love my empathy and compassion toward others
My cute little upturned nose
The smoothness of my skin

I'm in love with all the strange or quirky things about myself
Like how I have a note in my phone dedicated to dad jokes
Or how I laugh so hard I snort

I love that I can write this
That I can find things about myself to love
It took a while

A long journey
One filled with IVs and blood draws
Wheelchairs and EKGs

But I'm here now
I love me now
And why wouldn't I? There's so much to adore

I love my soulful eyes
I love my chestnut hair
I love my spunky curves
I love
I love
I love

Yep

I love myself now
Take that, demons

Because this is my love poem
Not to a boy or the world
But to me

The beach

Here I stand looking out towards the sea
The waves are teasing, but they can't reach me
The hard wet sand crunches beneath my feet
I wiggle my nose under the scorching sun's heat
I stand tall with my shoulders back
Watching as the sky gets tinted with black
I see the sea foam rolling across the top
The waves get bigger they just don't stop
The sky is gold with the evening light
I'm waiting just waiting for the day to be night
I wiggle my toes as they are licked by the waves
Watching as the light slowly drifts away

I want you to know,

I keep my phone on ring for you in the night.

Just in case you call me at 2 am,

Asking not to be alone.

Asking for someone to listen to you,

Asking for someone to sit there while you fall asleep.

We're just friends yeah,

But I keep my phone on ring for you.

I truly believe

That some of the strongest people in this world,

Are those with chronic illness,

And chronic pain.

Because

Every

Single

Day

Of my life,

I wake up in some sort of pain.

And

Every

Single

Day,

I make the conscious decision to get out of bed,

To go to school,

To put on that cute outfit,

To smile,

And to laugh.

And it's not me masking,

Or hiding my feelings,

It's me allowing myself to live.

It may not be a normal life,

Or the one I am expected to lead,

But it is still a life.

One that works for me.

So for everyone out there with chronic illness,

Or chronic pain,

I know what you're going through.

I see you,

And you're doing good.

This page is for you.

They know me as loud.

They know me as confident and bold,

A reflection of fire.

But not when it comes to you.

I am loud,

Yet with you,

I love in silence

Because theres not point of me yelling,

When you can't hear it

Why would I burn my light where you are blind?

I love you in silence.

Dot

Our lives
may just be a dot
on a timeline,but that's
our dot. And a dot is just a circle if
not filled. You get to decide how
to fill your dot. So make it one
worth remembering. That
is your purpose.

Puzzle pieces

He's not perfect
But then again neither am I
It's what we are
Imperfect pieces with jagged edges and complicated patterns
An ever-changing picture you can never quite see
Two people, so beaten by the world
And their own minds
So imperfect
Yet so perfect together
Because somehow
I have a dent to fit every one of his jagged edges
And every curve my pieces have fit so perfectly into his
We fit together in a way only we can see
We have ridges only we can feel
All we know is each other
And all I can see is the soul I love through his eyes

Sometimes,

When you're away from me,

I forget just how much I love you.

And then once I look into your eyes again,

It all comes flooding back to me in the sweetest river of memories.

It is undoubtedly,

My favorite feeling.

Whether it's a crack in the sidewalk,

Or a six foot trench,

You have to take the leap

And hope your feet hit solid ground on the other side.

You know,

They call us silly

They say we're naive to be this in love.

They call us dreamers

That our love story will never hold up

But they don't know.

This isn't la la land

Or moulin rouge

This is us.

We are dreamers

And we are silly and naive

But we're it together

The time we spend apart doesn't seem so scary when I know
we'll have eternity together.

Yes,

I know.

Every long song,

Every heart dangling poem,

Had you written between the lines.

Even if I thought it was someone else

It never was

It's you.

It's been you since seventh grade

And it will be you.

Until seventieth grade or whatever you call it when you die.

That's us.
Not Romeo and Juliet
Not Ross and Rachel
Us.
Let's write our story.

Men fear powerful women because they know, once the blinds are taken off, there is no stopping an angry horse from starting to run.

I want to be a mother

I am young and yet nothing sounds more appealing to me than the idea of cradling a life I made.

I want to be a mother

I want to lower my hand to my stomach and feel an entire life growing that will soon grow to be my entire life.

I want to be a mother

I want to be there for all the smiles and the laughs, the yelling and the crying.

I want to be a mother

I want to raise a child in a world that I helped make better.

I want to be a mother

I want to teach them all the things I was never taught and never shown.

I want to be a mother

I want to be responsible for a bright light in this world.

I want to be a mother

I want many someones to take care of and look after. Hearts to pour all my love into.

I need to be a mother.

I need to be a mother like I need to breathe. I wouldn't know how to not do it.

I'm not asking you to be my forever
But,
maybe you can be my right now?

This Is Poetry

They handed it to me and they said,
"This, this is poetry"
Edgar Allen Poe,
Shakespeare,
Dickinson.
Structured, strict rhyming schemes
Classes spent studying the ins and outs
Frustration with not knowing what it meant.
They said, "This is poetry"
But it is not my poetry.
My poetry is loud and clear,
A reflection of the person I am.
Maybe it is old poetry,
Maybe it is correct,
Maybe it is better.
But it is not mine.
I will write what is mine,
And pay grievance to those who question it.

Olive and Finn's Poem

Goodnight angel, I love you
More than anything and anyone
I hope that God blesses your dreams
And wakes you with the rays of the sun
Goodnight angel, I love you
Even higher than you can count
God has blessed me with a big heart
So my love for you will never run out

You

I used to think

Falling in love was this scary, horrible thing

Because I believed that everything that falls

Gets broken

But I didn't fall in love with you

I walked into it,

Knowing exactly where I was going

Because it was where I wanted to be

There were no cliffs

Or sharp turns

That took me by surprise

But there will be

And that's ok

I'm ready for them

As long as I'm with you, I could walk our path for days.

We are not promised tomorrow,
And we can't live in yesterday.
All we have is the now.
Be there for it.

Addiction

I know how silly it sounds
I know it's completely irrational to feel so young, especially
with you
But I just can't help myself
I'm addicted to you
I'm addicted to the way you make me feel
When you touch me
My nerves explode into fire
When you're near me
I have to fight the urge to pull you close and kiss you
endlessly
You make me feel complete
You make me feel whole
You make me feel safe
You feel like home.
I can always be myself around you
You make me feel more special than anyone or anything has
in my entire life
And I know that I said I'm over you
But I'm not.
And I'm not sure if I ever will be
Because loving you is like breathing
I do it a million times a day without thinking
It's easy
And calming

And natural.

My entire life I've shoved people away because I'm afraid of
this concept of love

But not you

It's not scary with you

It's safe

Because you're home for me

Here's the thing, I'm happy now.

I'm happy and healthy,

And I didn't get here with someone holding my hand and telling me I was gonna be okay.

I dragged myself out of those pits,

I sought out help,

I pushed myself to keep on going even when I was scared.

I got here through my own hard work.

So if my happiness

Or my cheerfulness

Or my energy

Annoys you

Or is too much,

You're just gonna have to deal with it.

Because I earned this peace.

And nobody's gonna take that away from me.

His picture might not be on these pages,
But his face is in every love poem I've ever written.

You will find me here.

Hiding under the lavender skies,

Dancing with the outspoken vines.

You will find me here.

Whispering secrets to the babbling brook,

Sharing wisdom with the old oak.

You will find me here.

Not in the busy streets with the busy people,

Or the black sky lit up only by city lights.

Instead,

You will find me here.

With the sunkissed grass underneath my heel,

And the fresh air blowing through my hair.

Here.

Where there is no noise,

No business,

No distractions,

In peace,

You will find me here.

I don't want a hot, steamy, tv show romance
I want someone who draws me a relaxing bath when they
know I've had a long day
Someone who will go on a Taco Bell adventure with me at
two am and not complain
Someone who touches me for the sake of comfort, not to get
something out of me
Someone who is open and honest with me even it's scary
Someone who lets me love them like I want to loved
I want the boom box outside of your window in the rain kind
of love
I don't want a passionate chapter
I want the story of a partnership.

Gardening

Only speak when you have something that needs to be said
Otherwise it's just filling the quiet air with meaningless words
The best thoughts sprout from the rich soil of silence.

I have Anorexia.

I have anxiety

I have depression,

I have PTSD.

It is a part of who I am.

But it is not,

Who I am.

Our experiences don't define who we are,

Our choices do.

Don't focus on the mistake,

But how you fix it.

It's not about the fall,

It's about the getting back up.

It's not our career,

Our sexuality,

Our gender,

Our age,

Our race.

It's about our voice and how we use it.

So if you have something to say,

Speak now or forever hold your peace.

Spring

Such is the allure
of the falling leaves
Dancing on the wind as it gently heaves
The soft music of the chirping birds
Its a beautiful melody,
Sung without words.
The vibrant colors of the blooming flowers
They never fade, even through the spring showers
The winter is a blank white canvas,
But then the brush covers the planet
With spring, comes the beautiful picture
But it'll be gone, with just a flicker.
Savor its beauty,
For it won't last long,
Keep in your heart the bird's beautiful song
Soak up the scent of the blooming blossoms
Drifitng in the air,
As the cold earth softens.
And when the sun sets,
And the birds start to rest,
After the sky turns black,
The beauty,
Will come back.

I want you,
I don't need you.

There's a difference.

(Reread Just Don't at the beginning)

No.

…

NO!

…

I didn't say everything
I needed to say
I have so much more songs
I'm meant to play
This isn't my last breath
My lungs still work
This isn't my death
My story just hurt

Please.
I'm not gone.

Author's Note

I hope that you connected with some of these poems, and I hope you don't. My intention with this book was not to make you sad or to make you feel a specific way. Poetry is a form of art that is all about perspective. I wrote this book for me. I connect with all of these pieces. But it is ok if you don't. It is ok to connect with some at one point in time, and different ones at another. I just want to give people, teenagers especially, a safe place to go, even if it's not an actual place. As a writer, my job is to make the trees smile at the new life I have given them through these pages. But your smile is just as rewarding.

About the Author

Coral Stewart is a seventeen-year-old high school graduate living in Ohio. She is close with her family, consisting of her mother, father, two older brothers, and many extended family members. She spent multiple years cultivating her first poetry manuscript and finalized it at age sixteen. She enjoys not only writing but also reading and many forms of creative expression, such as sketching, singing, acting, and jewelry making. She loves to fill her days with artistic activities and time with her loved ones, including her little beagle Gimli. No matter what these critical next steps of her life look like, she will always continue writing and sharing her story with the world.

About the Book

TBD is a powerful collection of poems with a wide range of emotions portrayed. From monologues of an ill mind to confessions of love, there is content for everyone to relate to. It is not just poetry. With three different sections– Pain, Healing, and Me –TBD sets the scene of a young girl fighting her way through the battles of life. It demonstrates the highs and lows of not only being a teen, but being a girl. But rest assured, anyone with the fundamental human experiences of love and suffering, can find solace within these pages.

www.ingramcontent.com/pod-product-compliance
Lightning Source LLC
Chambersburg PA
CBHW051832040426
42447CB00006B/489